Social Media Guru: Conquer the Challenge of Social Media Marketing and Drive Unlimited Traffic to Your Site

All rights Reserved. No part of this publication or the information in it may be quoted from or reproduced in any form by means such as printing, scanning, photocopying or otherwise without prior written permission of the copyright holder.

Disclaimer and Terms of Use: Effort has been made to ensure that the information in this book is accurate and complete, however, the author and the publisher do not warrant the accuracy of the information, text and graphics contained within the book due to the rapidly changing nature of science, research, known and unknown facts and internet. The Author and the publisher do not hold any responsibility for errors, omissions or contrary interpretation of the subject matter herein. This book is presented solely for motivational and informational purposes only.

Table of Contents

Facebook marketing 5

TWITTER MARKETING 16

LinkedIn Marketing 24

Instagram Marketing 36

Pinterest Marketing 46

'92% marketers in 2014 claimed that social media marketing was important for their business, with 80% indicating their efforts increased traffic to their websites.' - Hubspot

Social media marketing has been established by marketing pundits as a powerful fad that should be taken advantage of while it's still in the limelight. However, there are still quite a few entrepreneurs and marketers who feel bamboozled by this complex and complicated world. They still get lost when different social media platforms are being mentioned. While they could afford to remain clueless about the digital marketing world a decade or two ago, they can no longer afford it now. The pace of the digital world is increasing, and with it the need to stay on top of all the latest happenings.

According to Social Media Examiner,

"97% of marketers are currently participating in social media—but 85% of participants aren't sure what social media tools are the best to use."

This is one of the biggest dilemmas entrepreneurs new to the world of online marketing face. They're unaware of all the leading social networks that were embraced by marketing gurus half a decade ago. They desperately want to become a part of this exclusive group, but they're not even sure what their first step should be.

If you're one of them too, then don't worry. After reading this book, your journey towards dizzying heights of digital marketing success will be a breeze.

Facebook marketing

Old is gold. Well not old as such, but compared to all these new social media platforms popping up, Facebook is relatively older than the lot. However, like the adage goes, Facebook maybe old, but it's still a goldmine for marketers who know how to exploit it to its full potential. A huge goldmine, to be correct, as it currently has over 1.23 billion active users. Whoa.

Who's on it?

What started as a social network for college students has turned into a full-fledged marketing zone now. Everybody and their grandpas are on Facebook now. Even though a recent study by PEW showed that Facebook is far more popular with teens and tweens aged 18-24, you can still find a good amount of people in your preferred demographic to target. The minimum age to sign up is 13, so if your desired demographic is older than 13, you're good to go.

Is it really a marketer's dream come true?

Definitely. While many entrepreneurs (who provide products or services) dismiss Facebook as a consumer based platform for social media marketing, the truth is far from that. Facebook provides a plethora of marketing opportunities for all kinds of businesses – whether you're looking for paid advertising or free advertising; there's something for all.

So what are some of the main Facebook marketing features?

- **Pages:** Pages are quite similar to profiles, except they can be liked\followed by pretty much anyone unlike profiles. Furthermore, pages are usually made for businesses, organizations and public figures. They are also free to set up.
- **Groups**: Groups are forums where people can discuss various subjects; hence, groups have high levels of engagement. Groups make it easy to reach out to potential customers, and are free to set up as well.
- **Ads:** Ads can be created about a page, group or a specific event, etc. You can make ads as specific as you like. However, ads can get a little expensive.

How should you start?

Set Up your Page:

The first and foremost thing you need to do is set up your page.

1. Click on 'Create a Page' to get started.

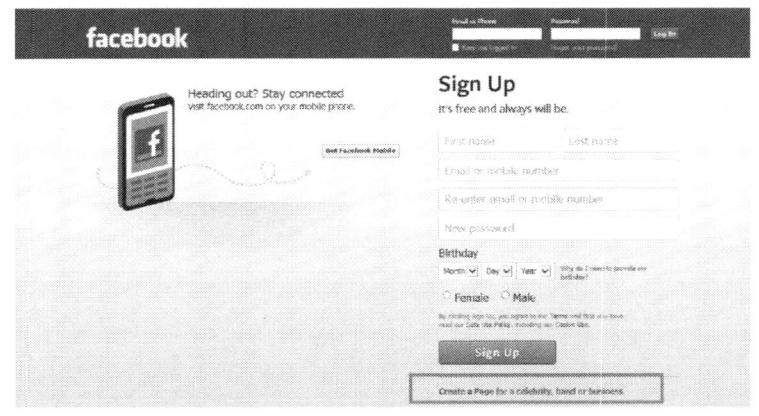

2. Choose from the available options depending on your business.

3. Once you choose the type of page you want to create, a little list will pop up in that box. Fill in the list with your business details, and click 'Get Started'.

4. Another form will pop up once you click 'Get Started'. Fill it up and click 'Save Info'.

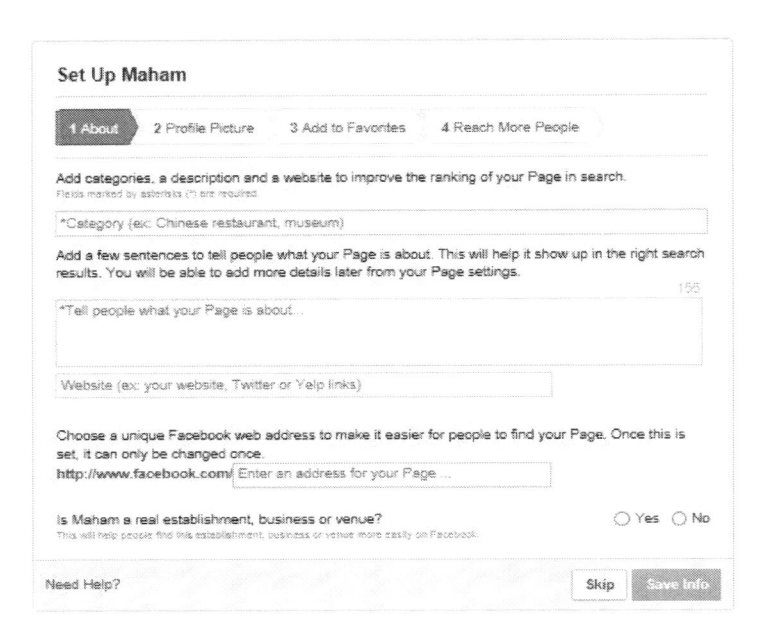

[Screenshot: Set Up Maham — Step 1 About form with fields for Category, description, Website, Facebook web address, and "Is Maham a real establishment, business or venue?"]

5. The next step is uploading your page's profile picture. So upload a picture that related to your business. A good idea would be to upload the logo of your company. Click 'Save Photo' once you're done.

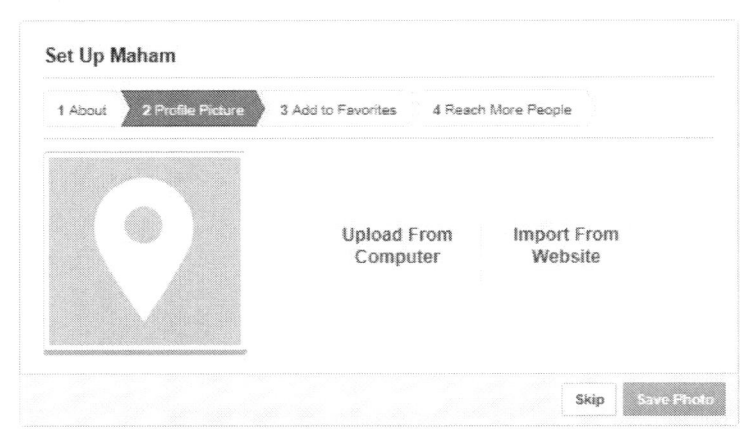

[Screenshot: Set Up Maham — Step 2 Profile Picture with options "Upload From Computer" and "Import From Website"]

6. The next step is adding this page to your favorites, so that you have easy access to it.

8

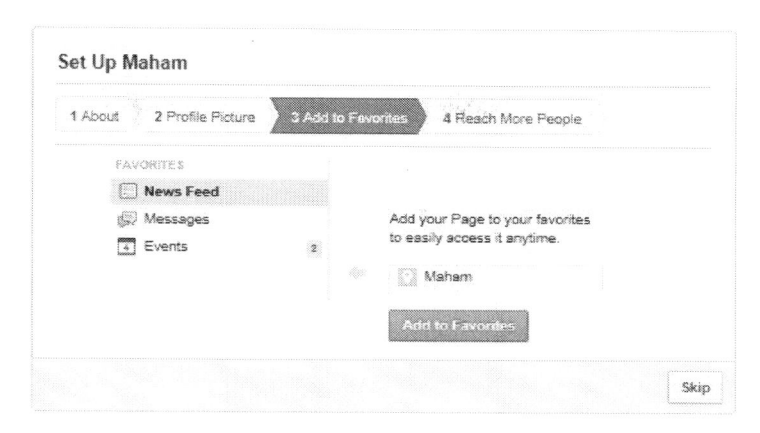

7. Last step is reaching out to more people. This basically consists of advertising your page, which we'll discuss in detail later on.

Voila, you're done. You've successfully set up a page for your business.

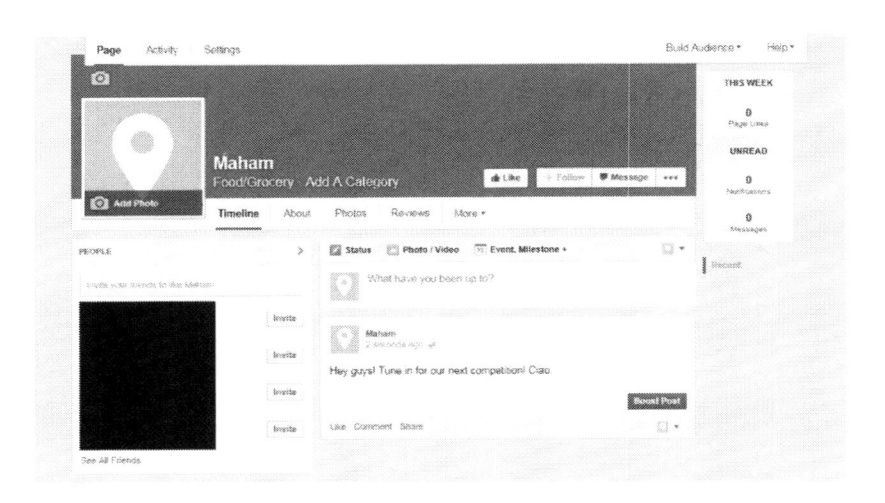

Figure out who your Audience is:

Once you've created a page for your business, you need to identify who's your audience and potential customer. Figuring out this is half the battle; the other half revolves around convincing them to use your product or services.

Start building your audience by:

- Asking existing customers to like your page and follow you on Facebook
- Inviting your family and friends to like your page
- Sharing the page
- Inviting your business contacts

Contrary to popular belief, your popularity does not depend on the number of likes you get; it depends on the quality of audience you've managed to attract. If you've managed to attract the right kind of audience, they will take over the legwork from you and market your brand by themselves by sharing your posts, etc. So in the end you need to attract the right kind of users, and then encourage them to stay with you to the very end.

But, how do you encourage them?

Posting Compelling content:

By posting compelling content you can ensure that your existing follower would return to your page and share, like and comment on the posts you upload. However, the keyword here is COMPELLING content. Content that provides value to your followers; content that bring out the fire within them, which would ultimately further your own marketing pursuits.

What kind of content is compelling content?

- One that has visuals.
  Tons and tons of visuals. Create infographics, videos, pictures, and pretty much any kind of visuals that would attract attention. Why? Because the brain processes visual information 60,000 times faster than it takes time for brain to decode text. Don't forget to check gifographics out as they're the latest IT thing to hit D-town.
- One that's published frequently and consistently.
  Consistency is a virtue, or it should be. Well, it sure is a virtue when you're trying to market your brand. However, don't forget that there's a fine line between producing posts consistently and spamming; you don't want to find yourself known as a spammer, so avoid that. Just make sure you post 2 to 3 times a day, and find out which of your posts are appealing to your crowd by checking the Page Insights option.
- One that allows you to respond well.
  Responding to customers is an old trick that does wonders to customer-client relationship. Read through the comments on each post, and try to answer your user's queries and questions. However, retain a bit of mystery by not acting as total pals – answer but don't answer too much.

Advertise, and advertise some more:

SPONSORED Create Ad

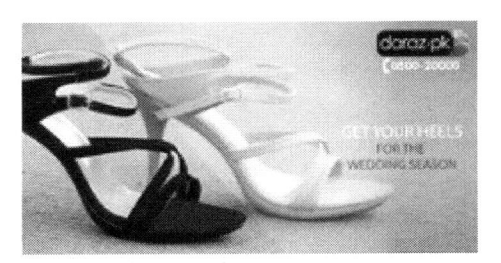

Click to Buy!
daraz.pk
Get the best selection from Women's heels only on Daraz.pk!
1,298,033 people like this

Ads are one of the most important parts of Facebook marketing. The only catch here is that you need to know how to do it right. There are several steps that eventually lead to a successful ad campaign.

Facebook advertising allows you to boost your page; however, you will need to a comprehensive company plan which provides a clear outline about your target audience and buyer persona. Once you've decided who your target audience is going to be and all other similar details, you need to decide what type of ad you'd like to create.

1. Click on 'Create Ad'. This action will take you to the next step that is choosing your ad campaign type.

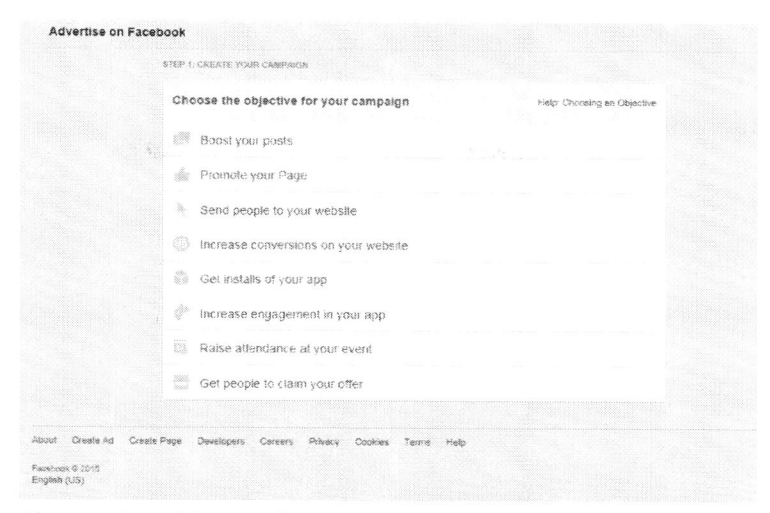

2. Choose the objective for your campaign. It depends on what you want to achieve from your ad campaign. Do you want more likes or more engagement? Etc. So choose from this list of available objectives, and choose wisely as this will shape up your entire campaign.

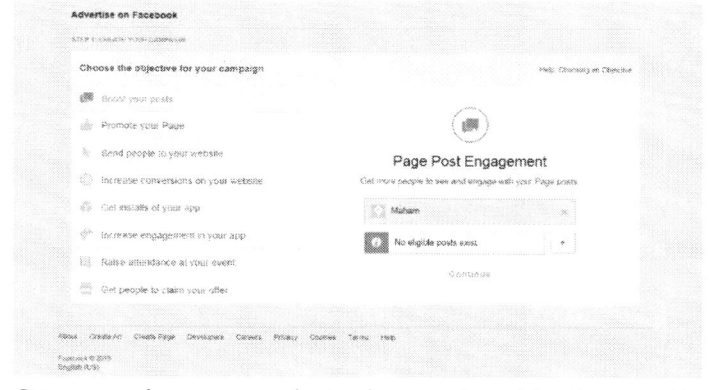

3. Once you choose your desired campaign objective, another screen will pop up right beside it asking for more details regarding your page and campaign. Each objective has a different kind of screen with different required details. So fill them up and place your order.

4. The next step is setting up a budget. There are several different ways you can choose to spend your Facebook marketing budget –

you can set a daily budget or a lifetime budget, use CPC (cost per click) or CPM (cost per thousand impression), etc. Facebook Ad manager will help you keep on top of all these details.

5. Promoted Posts is another great tactic of Facebook marketing. You can promote any post at any time to boost engagement. This can be especially useful when you're planning on running competitions, special offers, etc. All you need to do is click on the Boost Post option available at the bottom right hand corner. Next set your budget and choose the campaign type you require.

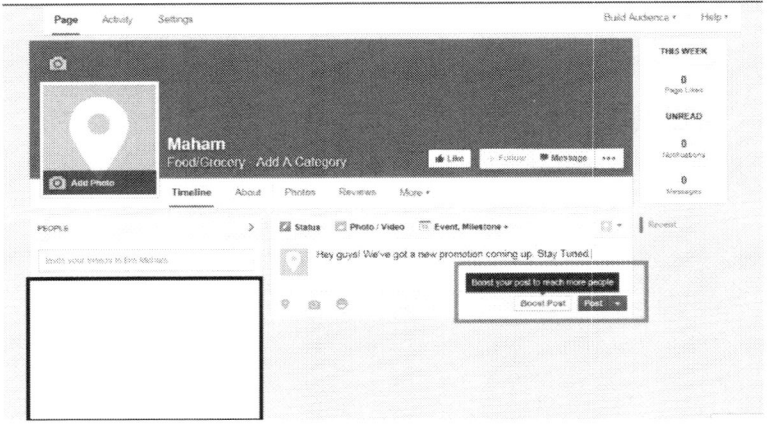

Once you've attracted the right kind of audience, and have a constant inflow of users liking your posts, use the ad create tool to reach the friends of the people who already like you and follow you. This is how you can transfer all the legwork to your users; they'll take over your marketing by sharing your posts and telling their friends to like your page. Never underestimate the power of word of mouth – it is still the most powerful marketing tactic out there.

One thing that you need to utilize completely is the targeting option that Facebook provides you with. You can target different audience type with different ads. This works really well because people are more likely to respond to a message that was specially crafted for them.

Fine-tuned targeting allows you to add a list of your existing customers to Facebook via 'Custom Audience' option, and then with the help of 'Lookalike Audiences' (an option found in the Ad create tool) you can find people who're similar to them. This cuts down your audience filtering time by a million times. Also, you can use 'Interest Targeting' (another option found in the ad create tool) to reach people who share similar interests to what your business offers.

Measure and Modify

Now that you've figured out what's working for and what isn't, you can easily maximize the influence of your posts and ads. There are several things you can do measure your success.

Page Insights allows you to measure your ad and posts success. Visit Page insights to find out which of your posts have been performing well, and which aren't; armed with this vital information you can tweak your marketing and content strategy to maximize the success. This page also lets you find out who's responding to your messages; this can help you figure out what kind of audience is your page attracting and which demographic is most engaged with your business.

Conclusion:

With over 864 million daily active users, it's almost impossible to ignore Facebook and the power it has over the masses. And as you've seen, building a presence on Facebook is quite easy; all you need to do is attract the right audience and then engage with them. Turn them into your loyal customers. So, go sign up and start marketing your brand.

TWITTER MARKETING

Hashtag and tweets – two things that instantly bring Twitter and a cute little bird to my mind. What started initially as a social media forum to rival Facebook, turned into a major goldmine for marketers and entrepreneurs. Now, social media marketing feels incomplete without Twitter in it.

And why wouldn't it? Twitter boasts of having 645,750,000 users, and over 58 million tweets per day. Exhausting, isn't it? However, these very same users, along with a couple of other unique factors, are the reason why marketers consider Twitter to be a major part of their marketing plans.

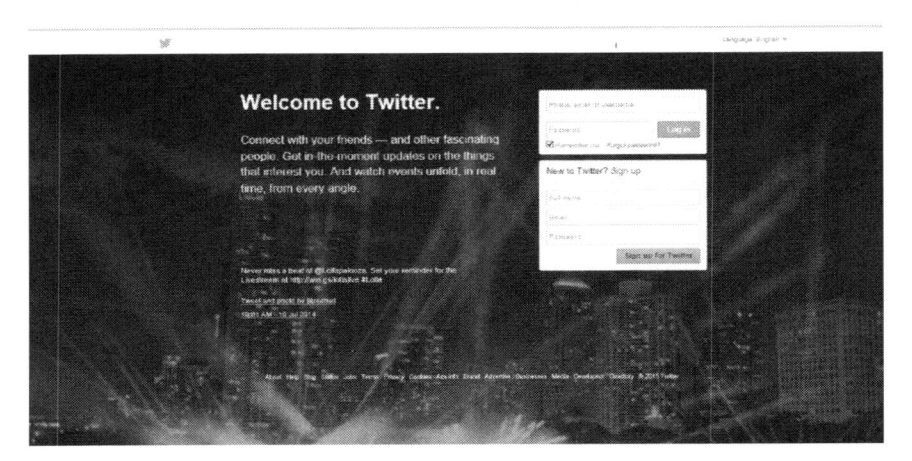

Getting Started:

The first and foremost thing you need to do is make an account. This account will then be the mediator between your brand and your potential customers. This account will singlehandedly make or break your brand on social media, so take each and every step very carefully, and refer back to your marketing plan and objectives each time you get stuck.

Set up your profile by signing up.

In order to start using Twitter to market your brand, you need to create an account. Creating an account is super easy.

1. Fill up the sign up form with the required details.

2. Upload a picture of yourself, or your business logo once your account has been created.
3. Add a short bio about your business.
4. Start following people and interacting with them.
5. Voila, you're done.

Important Twitter Profile Elements:

- Your Username

The @Twitter you see here is the username. The @username is what users on Twitter will reference you by. Also, the custom Twitter URL will also have that username.

Therefore, the need to use a relevant username for both your professional and personal account is immense; you don't want to end up with weird URL which does nothing to market your brand. Since you'll be using your Twitter URL in different marketing tactics, you need to have one that represents you and your brand perfectly. Furthermore, try to avoid using keywords as your username; there are several other ways of optimizing you profile with keywords, username is NOT one of them.

- Your Name

This is where your name comes in. Use this field for your business name or your own name only – don't try to add keywords here as it will make it difficult for users to search for you.

- Your Profile

There are several elements in your profile that, if used correctly, can optimize it and drive a lot of users to your profile.

1. Profile Photo – Make sure that you upload a picture that's either similar to the ones you've used in other social networks, or exact same. Exact same works better for obvious reasons; it makes it easier for people to follow you across all networks and it makes marketing your brand easier. For example, if someone's following your brand on Facebook, and if they come across your profile on Twitter, chances are that they'll start following it too. It works better in spots where only your picture is shown. So make sure you upload a picture that your followers recognize.

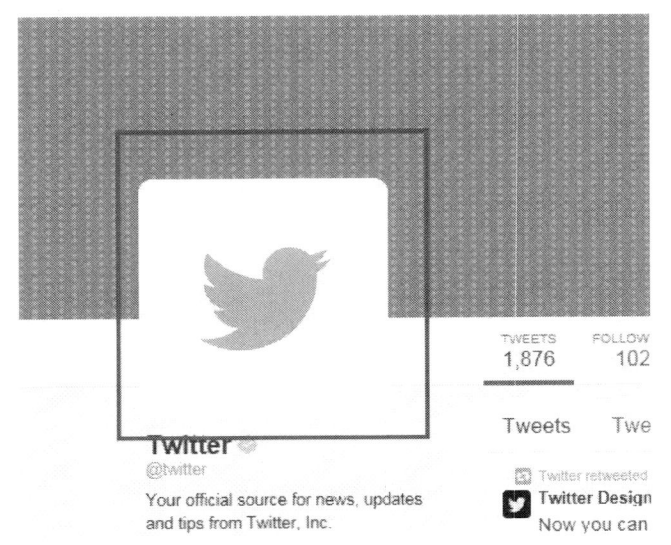

2. Header Image – Header image plays a very important part in marketing your business. It appears at the top-right part of your profile. There are several ways you can use header images to your advantage, however, try to add in an image that says something about your brand. Also, you need to keep in mind that if a twitter profile is viewed from mobile, the header image is all that shows; hence it should be something that your followers recognize.

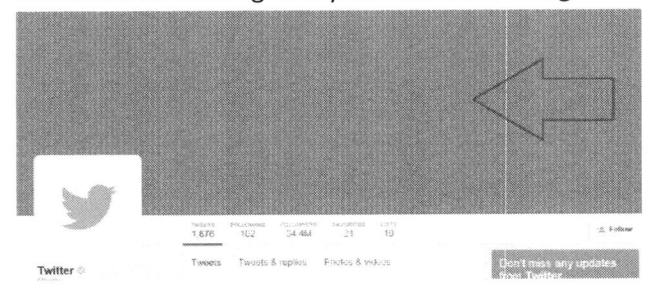

3. Profile bio – Your profile bio is a vital part of your profile. You can keyword optimize it, as keywords are searchable on Twitter. Include in keywords related to your business or yourself. Also, if you've got space left, add in your business URL as well, as it makes your profile stand out from the rest. Furthermore, you can also add in

@usernames in your bio in order to promote other accounts of yours. They'll be live linked, and so your employees can also promote your business from their personal Twitter accounts. A win-win for all!

4. Background Image – While not as important as your profile picture or your header image, background image plays a very important role as well. You can add a background image by going on the design section of the settings tab. Remember that background images should be under 2MB.

Growing your network:

The key to making it on social media networks is growing your network and reaching out to as many people as possible. With over 60% of the world population using internet, your potential customer base is vast; tapping into the global market is a lot easier now as well.

1. Follow button on your website can make all the difference
Add a follow button on your website to make it easier for people to follow you on Twitter. This will drive your website traffic to

your twitter account, and help you gain a large number of followers.

2. Your @username should be on everyone's lips
   A great way of broadening your network is by using your @username everywhere – all social media networks, business cards, store signage, etc. This will allow your existing customers to become acquainted with your Twitter profile, and they'll flock towards it in great numbers.

3. Sync your email contacts
   Sync your email accounts with your Twitter profile to start gaining followers, and to start following pages that lie in your area of interest.

Engaging followers and keeping them happy:

Engaging followers and keeping them happy will ultimately cut down your marketing job in half as these loyal followers of yours will take over the groundwork from you and start marketing your brand by sharing your posts. Therefore, it is essential that you interact with your followers. There are several ways of engaging with followers;

1. Answer their queries and questions.

2. Conduct creative competitions and giveaways.

> CC Competitions retweeted
> **Teletext Holidays** @TeletextHoliday · 8h
> It's Bamboozle #ThrowbackThursday #competition time - just RT or Fav by 4pm for a chance to win a £20 voucher!
>
> 13C Teletext 390 Jan08 11:00:00
> Which reality tv series returned to our screens last night?
> RT Big Brother   FAV The Apprentice
> REPLY WITH YOUR ANSWER BY 4PM:
> Amazon Voucher!
> 586 100   View more photos and videos

3. Tweet with your followers and other users in real time events such as premiers, show finales, etc.

4. Feature events that are popular in your industry and will appeal to a huge amount of your followers.
5. Stay on top of latest events, and tweet about them.

Conclusion:

In this dog eat dog world, you need to have an edge over your rivals; you can no longer be content with what you're doing in terms of marketing your brand, you need get proactive and find ways to get an edge over your rivals. You can now no longer afford to avoid the many ways of digital marketing, so take your first step in this world and start making your presence known to billions of people. They're all waiting to hear from you.

LinkedIn Marketing

"Start your professional profile. Set yourself up for success. Connect with people you know. Keep in touch and find opportunities. Find news and insights."

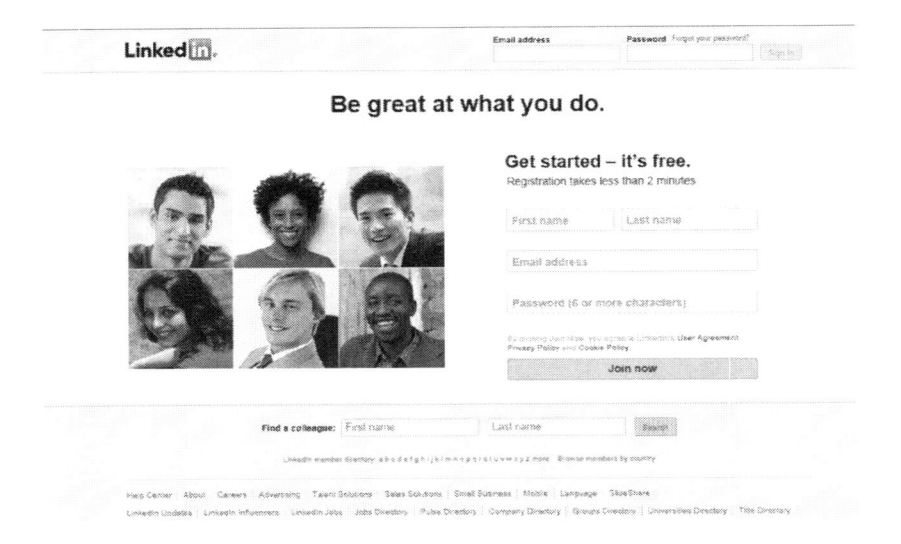

LinkedIn is one of the most powerful marketing tools of this decade. What started in 2003 as a business oriented social network has now turned into one of the greatest business tools that most entrepreneurs swear by. Not only does it provide a plethora of opportunities to businesses that are looking for an increase in their traffic, but also allows individuals to market their skills and find prospective clients.

Taking the first few steps with LinkedIn:

Just like every other social network, you need to create an account to begin this exciting journey. Creating an account on LinkedIn is just filling a long form with all your business and personal details; but then again since these very details are the reason prospective customers and clients will come knocking to your door, it makes great sense to take some time out and create a perfect LinkedIn profile.

Creating your Profile:

1. Fill up this form to get started. Click 'Join Now' once you're done.

> # Get started – it's free.
> Registration takes less than 2 minutes.
>
> [First name] [Last name]
>
> [Email address]
>
> [Password (6 or more characters)]
>
> By clicking Join Now, you agree to LinkedIn's User Agreement, Privacy Policy and Cookie Policy.
>
> **Join now**

2. Clicking 'Join now' will take you to another screen which will contain another form where you need to fill in the required details.

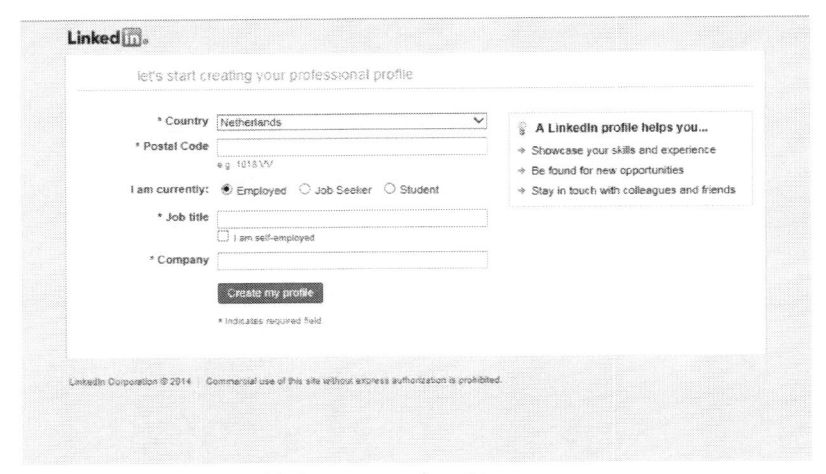

Click 'Create my profile' once you're done.

3. Woohoo, you're done. Yes, it's really this simple.

   You've successfully made a profile; however, your work here isn't done. Now you need to start setting up your professional profile.

Setting up your Profile:

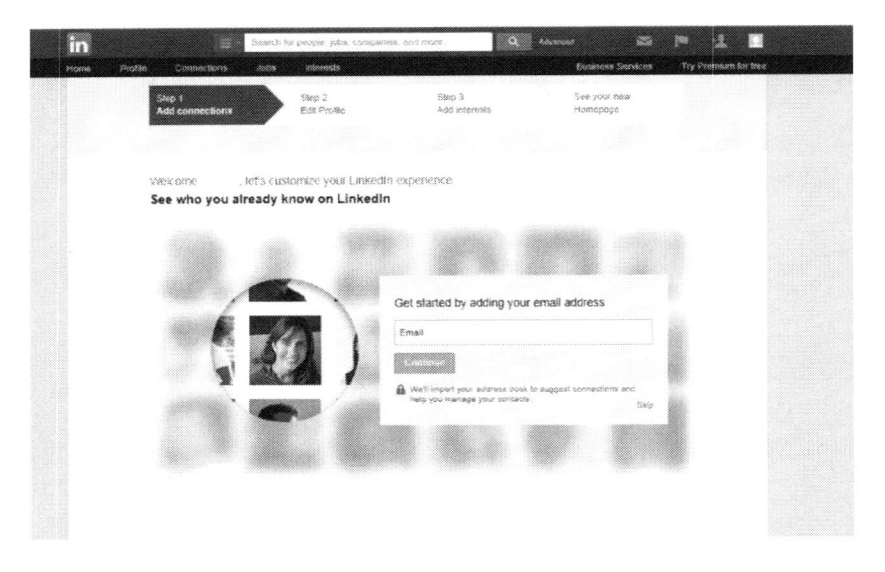

Now that you've created your profile, you need to set it up in a professional manner and add in all the details that a prospective customer or a client would want to know in order to avail your services. LinkedIn makes it easy for us, by taking us through the 3 main tasks of setting up a profile.

STEP 1 – ADD CONNECTIONS

This step entails growing your network. There are several ways of growing your network.

1. The first is by finding contacts through your email address book. This is one of the easiest ways of adding connections.

   You can also connect with your fellow colleagues at your previous or even current organizations. Or, you can add in alumni from your college.

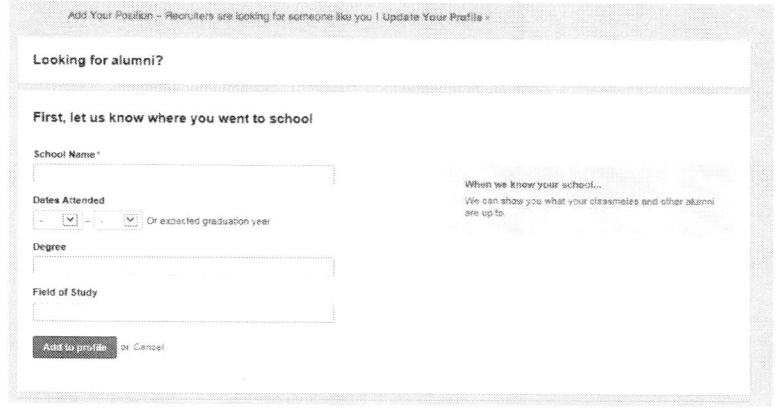

2. LinkedIn also provides you with a 'people you may know' browser. You can use this browser to find people in your network and add them to your LinkedIn profile.

3. Now that you've added everyone you can think of, you can start sending out invitations to other people.

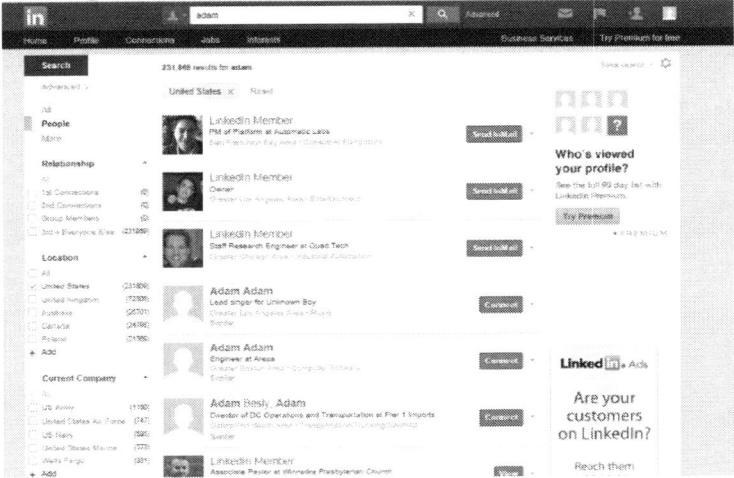

However, keep in mind that LinkedIn only encourages you to send out invitations to people you know, hence, sending out random invites to people who're likely to flag you will just result in your account being suspended. So be careful who you send out an invite to.

As you start sending out invites and adding connections, you'll see tiny annotations by people that show your connection to them. There are 4 different kinds of annotations:

- 1st degree connection – This annotation is given to people who're a part of your network.
- 2nd degree connection – This annotation is given to people who're connected to people in your network.
- 3rd degree connection – This annotation is given to people who're connected to your 2nd degree connection.

- Group – This annotation is given to people who're in a group you're part of, too.

4. The next way of connecting with people is via groups. Groups are places where people can take part in discussions, talk to each other about similar interests, etc.; basically like a forum. If you send out an invite to someone in your group just mention that you know them through a certain group. However, it's better if you've interacted with them before sending out an invite; you really don't want someone to flag your invite – trust me on this one. Also, sending out a custom message before connecting is a great way to engage with them and build a level of trust.
5. Another way of adding connections is by adding your LinkedIn profile link to your blog or website, and on other networks where you're given an opportunity to add this link such as Google+, etc. Also, posting snippets from your LinkedIn profile, sharing your LinkedIn profile URL on different social media platforms where you've already got a nice following can also help you get connections.

STEP 2 – EDIT PROFILE, STEP 3 – ADD INTERESTS

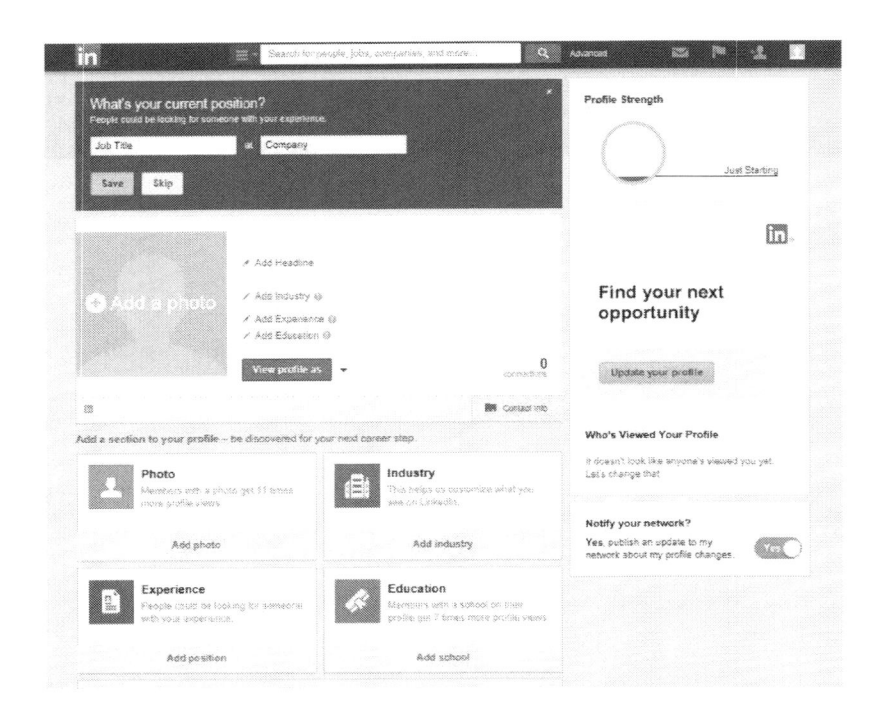

The next step is editing your profile and describing your professional skills in order to lure prospective customers\clients.

- Click on the 'Profile Tab' and then 'Edit Profile'.

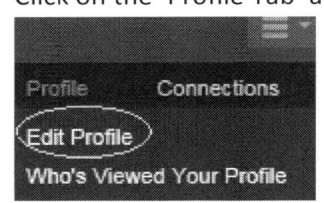

Now you've got your profile in front of you. There are several elements in your profile that you need to fill in in order to completely define your professional skills.

1. Name – Just write your full name in it. Yup, that's it.

2. Headline – Your headline is one of the most important elements of your profile as it comes up in several places – messages,

invitations, search results, employee listing, etc. Therefore, you're free to keyword optimize it so that users can easily search you.

3. Summary – This section lets you describe your professional expertise and experience. LinkedIn has also introduced a media section here, which allows you to upload videos, slideshows, etc. describing your experience.

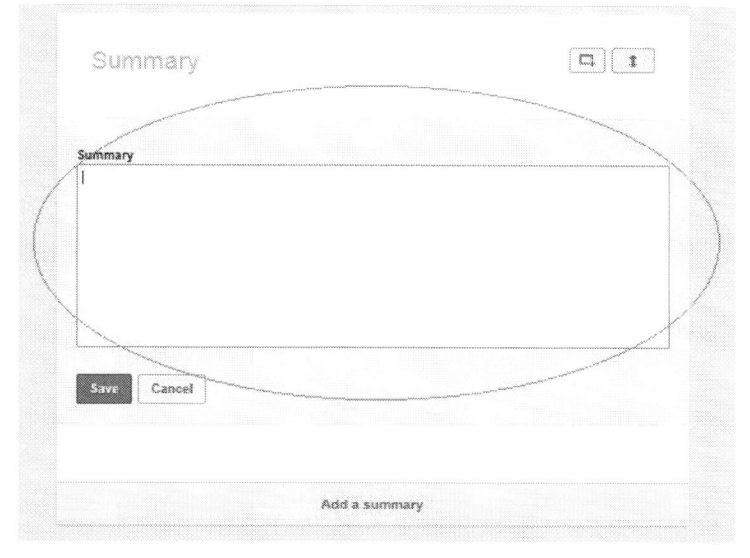

4. Current and Past Job Experience – This is another section where you can add keywords as LinkedIn uses it to determine which keywords should your profile be ranked for.

5. Skills and Endorsements – You can add in your skills her to be endorsed by others. Endorsements are relatively easier to get than recommendations as connections are automatically prompted to endorse you by LinkedIn when they visit your profile.

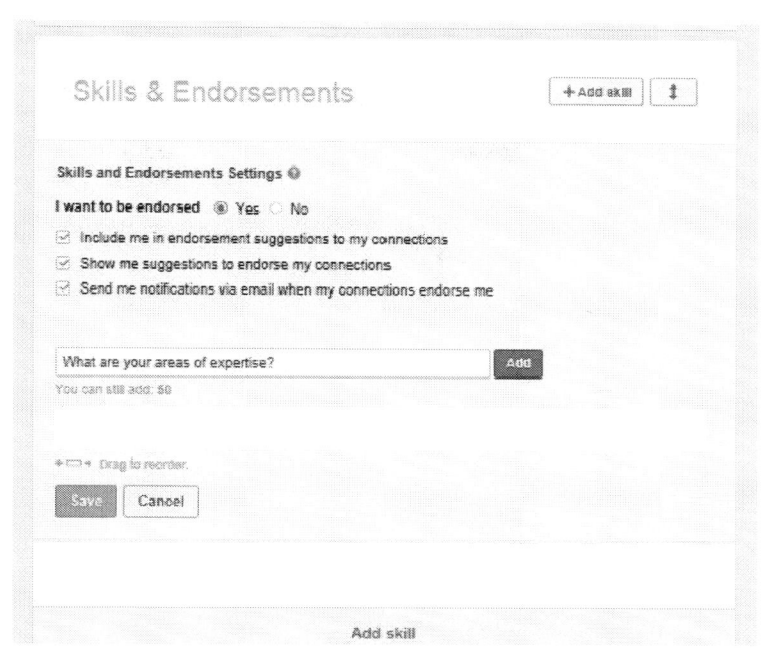

6. Additional Sections – There are several additional sections as well, so make sure you browse through them thoroughly.

Add summary	Add skills
Language This can help you find a new job, get a promotion, or transfer overseas. Add language	**Volunteering Experience** 1 in 5 managers hired someone because of their volunteer experiences. Add volunteering experience
Volunteering Opportunities Non-profit organizations could be looking for someone like you. Add volunteering opportunities	**Organizations** Add more color to your professional identity to show who you are. Add organizations
Honors & Awards Show the recognition you've earned. Add honors & awards	**Test Scores** Here's another way to show your accomplishments. Add test scores
Courses Showing more information about your background will help you get found for more opportunities. Add courses	**Patents** Showcase your innovation and expertise. Add patents
Causes you care about Show the causes that matter to you. Add causes	**Supported Organizations** Add more color to your professional identity to be found for opportunities. Add supported organizations
Projects This helps show your skills, experience, and people you've worked with. Add projects	**Publications** Publications are a great way to show off your professional accomplishments. Add publications

Pro Accounts:

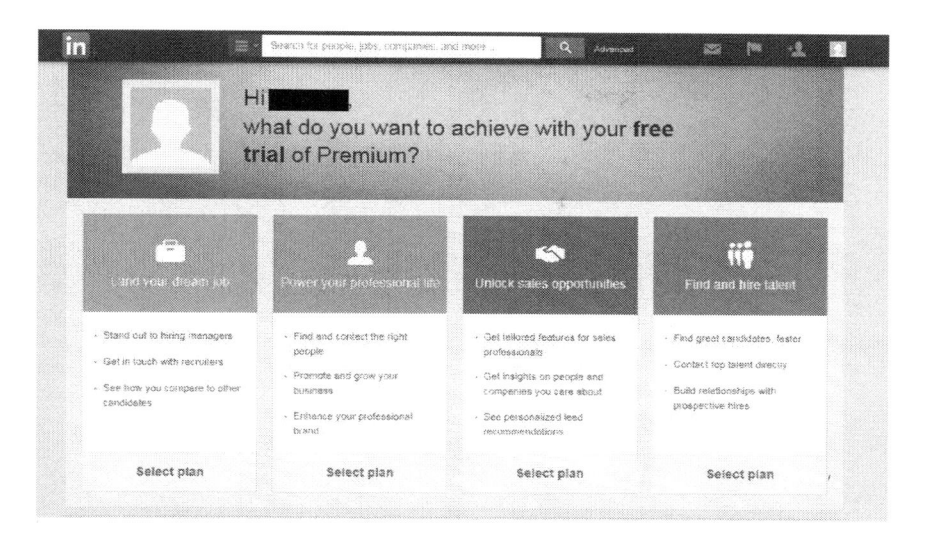

LinkedIn offers premium accounts to entrepreneurs searching for a bit more. There are 4 plans available; each offering different features and different benefits.

- Job Seekers premium account: $29.99 / month.
- Business Plus premium account: US$59.99 / month
- Sales Plus premium account: US$59.99 / month
- Recruiter Lite premium account: US$119.95 / month

Conclusion:

This should allow you to plant your feet firmly in the LinkedIn world and progress towards success. So take the first step and make your LinkedIn account; it all gets easier after that. Also, remember to engage with people, that's the main reason LinkedIn is so popular; it allows you to engage and interact with like-minded people.

Instagram Marketing

Visuals have always had an edge over words, and the rising popularity of Pinterest and Instagram is the evidence of this very fact. There's a reason why over 300 million users are completely and irrevocably addicted to Instagram. Everybody seems to be in a race to put up selfies, breakfast meal pictures, weird shaped clouds images, and what not.

1. 67% of consumers consider clear, detailed images to carry more weight than product information or customer ratings.
2. Visual content drives engagement. In fact, just one month after the introduction of Facebook timeline for brands, visual content -- photos and videos -- saw a 65% increase in engagement. (Simply Measured)
3. 67% of consumers consider clear, detailed images to be very important.

Within 4 years, Instagram's popularity has skyrocketed; it is now one of the top social media platforms. While its registered users (200 million monthly active users) may be less than that of other leading social networks, the engagement rate is quite possibly the highest out of all platforms. A recent study conducted by rock band Paramore's social media accounts showed that a similar picture, which was posted on all leading networks, displayed the following results.

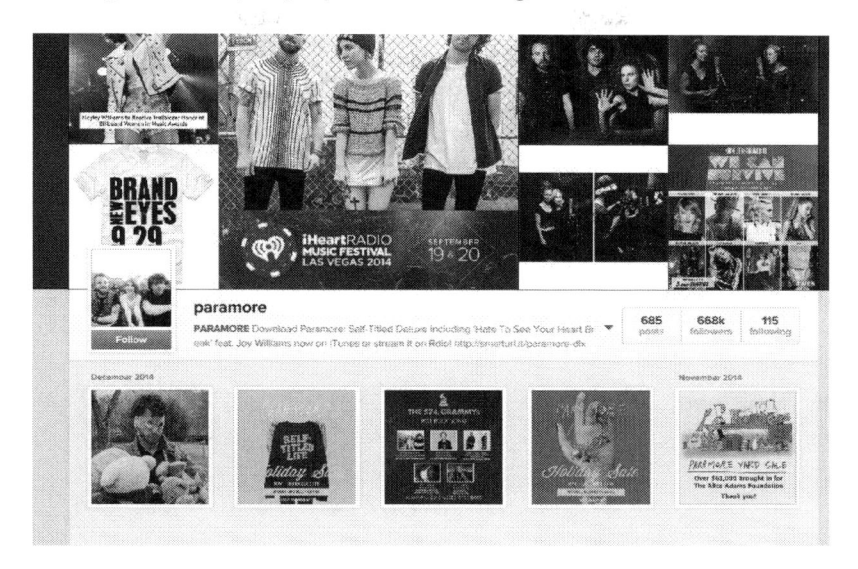

- Facebook Fan Page (3,200,000 fans) – 9,405 likes
- Twitter (3,350,000 followers) – 433 retweets and 289 favorites
- Instagram (360,000 followers) – 52,237 likes and 315 comments

This shows that despite having the least number of followers, the picture posted on Instagram received the highest number of likes, which in turn means the highest number of engagement.

Let's get started:

Just like other social networks, you need to create an account on Instagram to start using it. However, unlike other social networks, like Pinterest and Facebook, Instagram doesn't differentiate between individual and business accounts.

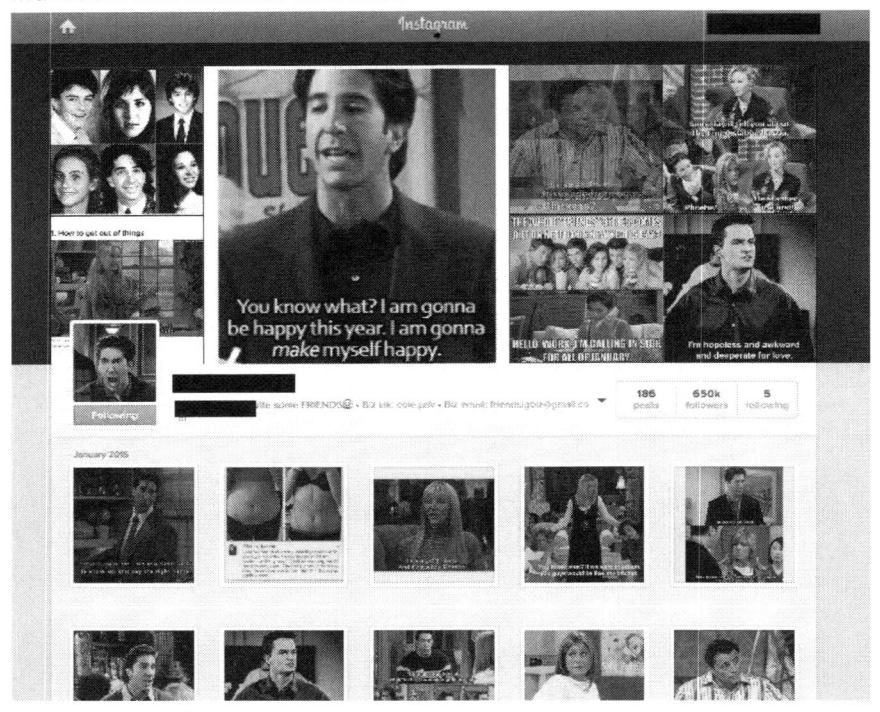

1. Create an account through your smartphone.

2. Once you've created an account, you can easily use it through your laptop or pc.

3. You don't need to make separate business and personal accounts, as Instagram doesn't discriminate between business and individual accounts. All accounts are same.

4. You can also quite easily change your profile\account name if you want, and as many times as you want. Furthermore, you can add underscores (_) and periods (.) in your username as well.

5. The next thing is selecting your profile photo. This image cannot be zoomed when users click, and it will be the only people that

represents your business so make sure you upload one that your followers are recognize.

6. You only get 150 characters to write a blurb in your profile, so use these limited characters wisely. Write a slogan pitch, etc. but remember to keep it simple.
7. You can add in an outward link in the profile bio as well, so use it wisely, as you're not allowed to add outward links anywhere else in your profile.

Creating posts that go viral:

Now that you've created an account, you need to start posting pictures that would attract users. There are two things you need to focus on while marketing your brand on Instagram; quality content and maximizing engagement. If you've got a thousand followers and just 50 or so likes on your pictures, then you should be aware that you're doing something wrong. Engagement is the keyword on Instagram.

So how can you make sure that the post you're creating will enjoy a high engagement rate?

- #UseHashtags

39

This is the decade of hashtags. What started with Twitter has now been embraced by all platforms. While not the newest thing to hit D-town, hashtags are definitely one of the most popular features.

So what are hashtags? They're basically words, or phrases that follow the # symbol. For example, #Newyork, #Instagram #NoFilter, #business, etc. When users search for a particular hashtag, Instagram shows them all pictures that were posted with that hashtag, hence it groups together pictures that have the same hashtag.

There are two ways of using hashtags which will maximize the visibility of your posts.

1. Use the trending hashtags and be part of a discussion with 2 million participants. However, unlike other platforms, Instagram doesn't show you the trending the hashtags, but you can use the trending hashtags from Twitter and Facebook on
Instagram. While the trending hashtags may not be

related to your business, it will increase your post's visibility and allow it to be displayed in front of a huge audience which has the potential to become future customers.

2. Come up with your own hashtag and spread it far and wide. Kit Kat has used this strategy very effectively. Its famous slogan 'Have a break' is now a very popular hashtag used by huge number of people on Instagram. The Kit Kat marketing team created their brand hashtag and encouraged followers and other users to post pictures with this hashtag. The popularity of this hashtag gained a lot of momentum, and soon people started posting personal content with this hashtag.

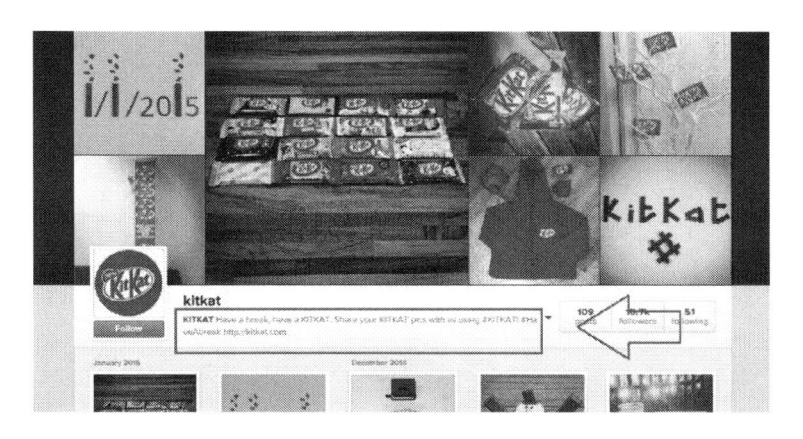

Coming up with hashtags, especially one's that'll go viral is not easy; therefore, you can use the iconoquare tool (iconosquare.com) to figure out which hashtags would go best with your business. All you need to do is enter in a keyword related to your business and it will come up with a list of hashtags related to that keyword and their associated volume.

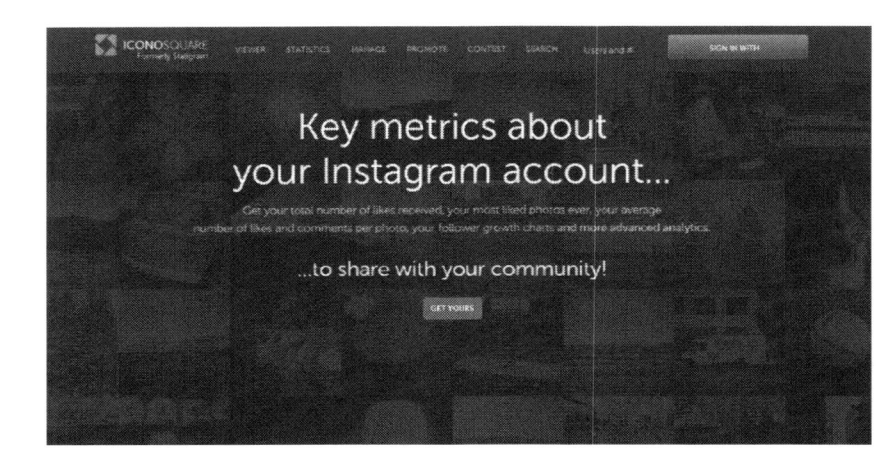

- **Filters**

Instagram provides users with several different filters to choose from. Since it's a picture centered platform, the filters are a huge bonus for users. They allow users to give a little edge to their pictures. However, as an entrepreneur who's trying to market their brand, try not to use too many filters unless the picture quality is poor; filters can be an excellent way to convert poor quality pictures into edgy ones.

The ten most used filters are:

1. Normal / No filter
2. Earlybird
3. X-Pro II
4. Valencia
5. Rise
6. Hefe
7. Amaro
8. Hudson
9. Brannan
10. Nashville

- **Push posts to your other social network accounts**
  Social media marketing can get tedious and time-consuming, therefore in order to avoid wasting time posting the same posts on each of your social media account, Instagram provides you with the option of linking posts to other network accounts. All you need to do is tap on the account from the 6 social networks available, and your post will automatically be posted on the other accounts.

  These are 6 social networks you can push your posts to.

  1. Facebook
  2. Twitter
  3. Tumblr
  4. Flickr
  5. Foursquare
  6. Mixi

  Also, if you've got a lot of fan following on other accounts, and are in dire need of a little traffic on your Instagram account, this option will also open the traffic doors for you as Instagram posts which are posted on other networks are displayed as coming from an Instagram account.

- **Embed on website**
  Along with social media networks, Instagram also provides you with an option to embed posts on your website, thereby driving your website traffic to your Instagram account. A super easy tactic that is very popular among marketers.

- **Likes, Comments and Follows**
  You can use likes, comments and follow option to your advantage as well. All you need to do is enter in a hashtag related to your business field, go on the pictures that are displayed and engage;

like them, comment on them and follow their pages. This will allow other people to view you and follow you. However, don't follow too many people unless you've got as many or more followers too; the profile looks bogus otherwise.

There are two Instagram rules that you need to remember when going on a liking, commenting, following spree; Instagram only allows 50 comments per hour, and 350 likes per hour in order to filter spam.

- **Connect with influencers**
    A very effective way of growing your fan following is by connecting with influencers of your industry. Due to the high engagement levels of Instagram, connecting with influencers can easily make your marketing campaign a raving success. There are two kinds of influencers on Instagram:
    1. Celebrities: Connecting with celebrities is very difficult and expensive. Unless you're an advertising agency that is prepared to empty there bank vaults, you don't have much chance with them
    2. Users with huge fan following: You should be on a lookout for users with over 25000 followers. There are two main ways to connect with them.
        a. Send them an email
        b. Send a direct message

    Don't forget to have a proper strategy before you go knocking on influencer's doors. Make a spreadsheet of all the influencers you want to extend a friendship hand towards, and then start messaging them.

Conclusion:

Instagram is a platform that is greatly misunderstood by most entrepreneurs and thought off as a plaything for teens and tweens; however, it's anything but. While with the latest picture obsession,

Instagram does appeal, it does have tons of potential for marketers as well. So, make sure you fully utilize the plethora of benefits this platform has.

Pinterest Marketing

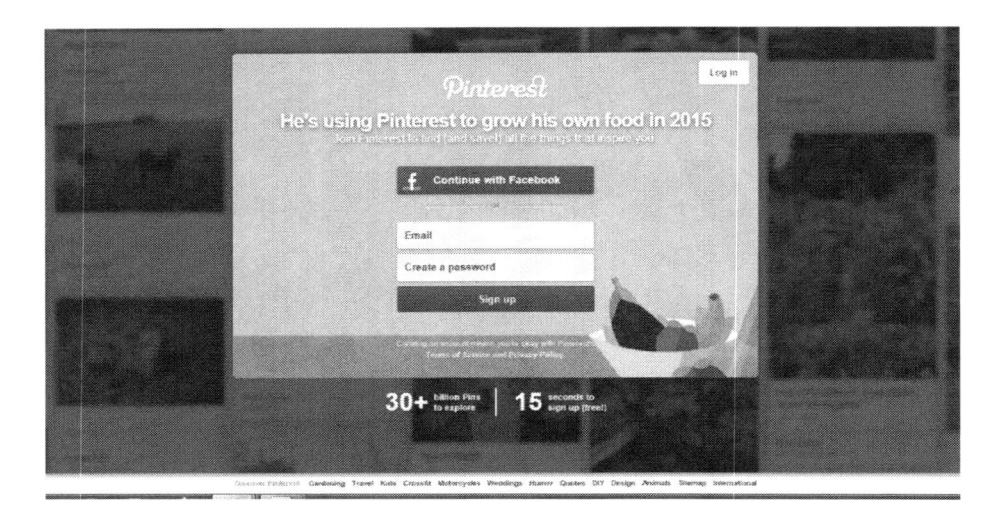

Pictures are worth a thousand words; an adage that rules over the digital marketing world. Visuals truly are worth a lot more than words, and platforms such as Pinterest are a witness to this. What launched in March 2010, as a social networking site in which conversations consisted mainly of pictures, has become one of the fastest growing websites and a heaven for marketers. Users no longer need words to express themselves when pictures can do a much better – and faster – job. So why has Pinterest gathered so much interest? Why are people eager to be part of the Pinterest bandwagon?

What makes Pinterest a perfect arena for entrepreneurs to market their business?

"90% of information transmitted to the brain is visual. Visuals are processed 60,000X faster in the brain than text". - Zabisco

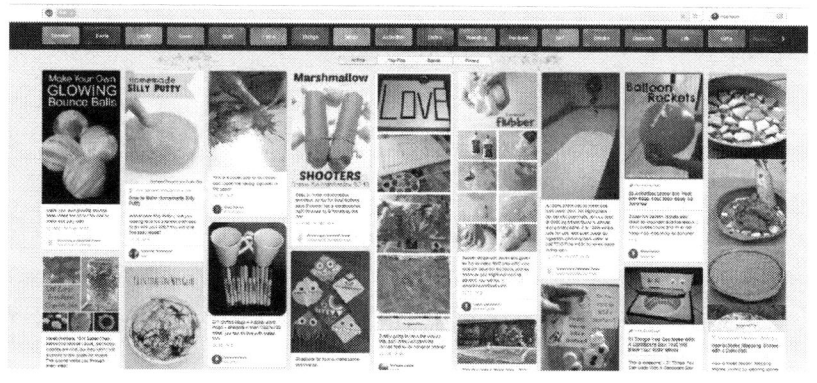

In an era where pictures speak louder than words, selfies are the newest obsession, and everyone and their dogs own a DSLR, platforms such as Pinterest enjoy a lot of positive acclaim. A recent study showed that,

"Pinterest generated more referral traffic for businesses than Google+, YouTube, and LinkedIn combined" — Shareaholic

There has to be a reason why a relatively new platform garnered approval from various renowned marketers. While it is true that the main focus of Pinterest is to provide a social networking platform where people can post, share and pin their favorite pictures, it is not merely there to provide entertainment; rather, marketers can utilize this very feature of this platform to further their marketing quests as well.

So, how does Pinterest work?

Pinterest is basically a huge virtual board with over a million pictures. It lets people look over captivating picture, choose ones they like, comment under them, and pin them in their own pinboards so that they can share their new findings with their friends and followers. However, the keyword here is captivating pictures. As a marketer you get just one chance per picture to appeal your audience and strike gold. Therefore you need to ensure that the picture is captivating enough to get repinned and shared.

That's the trick to getting it right on Pinterest – getting your images repinned over and over again.

Now, why would you to want to get your images repinned and shared across Pinterest? Because each image carries an external site – which in this case would your website, blog, etc. – and clicking on the image would take the user to that site. This would increase the traffic to that site, and turn unaware users into potential and loyal customers. Furthermore, if users like what they see on your pinboards they also have the option of embedding those pins on their blogs and websites – thereby playing a vital role in your business's marketing. Either way, it all comes down to that one captivating picture.

Starting a successful Pinterest journey

- **Make an account**
  Like in every other social media platform, you need to make an account which will represent you and your business.
    1. Go to - https://business.pinterest.com/en

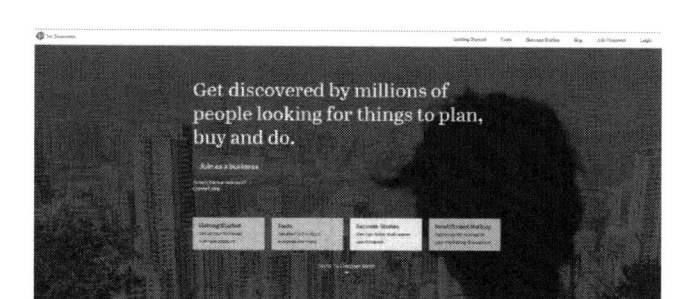

2. Click 'Join as a business'. Or if you already have an account on Pinterest, you can easily convert it into a business account by clicking on the 'Convert Now' option.
3. Fill the following form up.

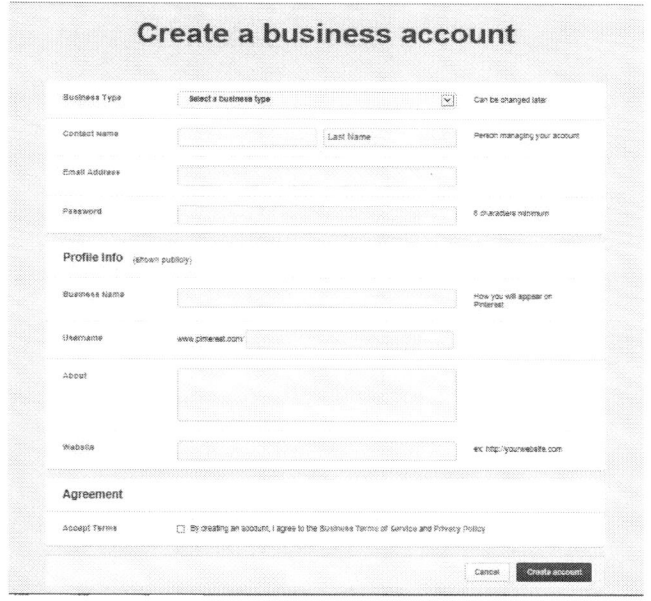

4. Click on 'Create Account' once you're done.
5. Pick themes in which you're interested. A good strategy would be to choose ones that relate to your business.

6. Aaaaand, you're done. Your profile's all set up.

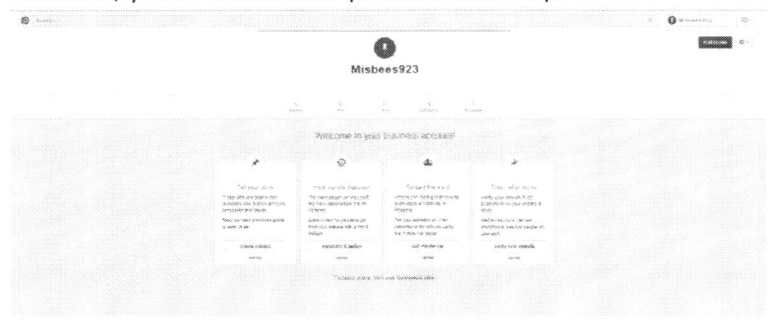

You can link your Pinterest profile to your email which is also used for Twitter; this will allow you to share images on both the social media networks. Also, add the Pinterest button to your blog, portfolio, website, email, etc. to help you in promoting your business.

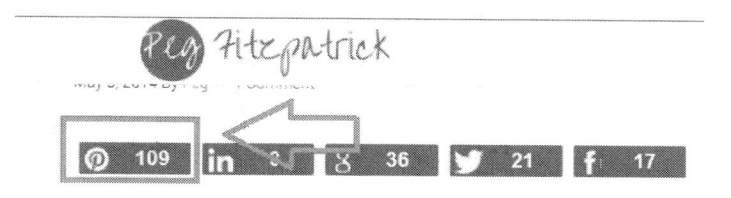

Going beyond the obvious – tips and tricks to accelerate your Pinterest marketing success

In order to have an edge over your rivals you need to do a little something extra. Mediocre no longer does the job – you need to go far and beyond what everyone is doing to take the final step of success. Here are some ingenious tips and tricks that can make this task a whole lot easier:

1. Use keywords in your board titles
   Using keywords in your board titles allows interest to determine you accordingly; therefore when users search for a keyword you've used, the search results would show them your board as well. Hence, keyword optimization can do wonders for your brand if used effectively.

2. Build links back to your website
   Links are a great way to drive traffic. Pinterest allows you to add links in pin description and in the source of the pin. So make sure you utilize this opportunity wisely, and send a truck full of traffic to your website.

3. Tall, vertical Images get all the traffic
   Vertical images are Pinterest's favorite; so make sure that the images you pin are long and narrow and utilize maximum space. This will not just get them noticed, but they also look visually appealing.

4. Start a tips board
   Tips boards are a great way of establishing you as an expert. They also invoke curiosity in users, as useful information is always in great demand. So, find a creative way through which you can share tips and strategies with users in your industry. Trust me, this tactic will reap great rewards.

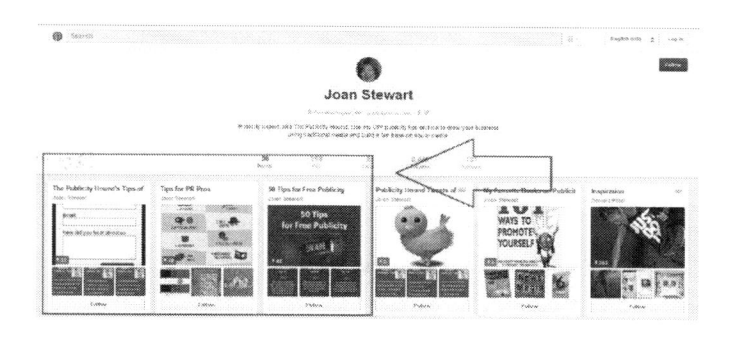

5. You can never go wrong with Collaborative boards
Collaborative boards are basically boards which you share with other users. Like a group of users will collaborate together and create a board. If you're the owner of the group, you're only allowed to choose the cover photo. These boards help newbies plant their feet firmly in this arena; however, you need to be careful not to choose pinner who don't share your interest, or your business's interests, as all the images pinned in that group will be visible on your Pinterest presence as well.

Conclusion:

Visuals have taken over the digital marketing world by a storm, and Pinterest is quite ahead in this race. Entrepreneurs and marketers can no longer avoid Pinterest and dismiss it as frivolous; it has a great amount of potential for business and personal branding, so make sure you utilize all that it has to offer.

Manufactured by Amazon.ca
Bolton, ON

33686875R00031